EXPLORING CAREERS

Writer

Peggy J. Parks

**KIDHAVEN
PRESS**™

THOMSON

™

GALE

San Diego • Detroit • New York • San Francisco • Cleveland
New Haven, Conn. • Waterville, Maine • London • Munich

© 2004 by KidHaven Press. KidHaven Press is an imprint of The Gale Group, Inc., a division of Thomson Learning, Inc.

KidHaven™ and Thomson Learning™ are trademarks used herein under license.

For more information, contact
KidHaven Press
27500 Drake Rd.
Farmington Hills, MI 48331-3535
Or you can visit our Internet site at http://www.gale.com

LIBRARY OF CONGRESS CATALOGING-IN-PUBLICATION DATA

Parks, Peggy J., 1951-
  Writer / by Peggy J. Parks.
    v. cm.—(Exploring careers)
  Includes bibliographical references and index.
  Contents: Types of writers—What it takes to be a writer—What writers do—Meet a writer.
    ISBN 0-7377-2069-7 (Hardback : alk. paper) 23.70
  1. Authorship—Juvenile literature. [1. Authorship—Vocational guidance.
2. Vocational guidance.] I. Title. II. Exploring careers.
(KidHaven Press)
  PN153.P39 2004
  808'.02—dc22
                                                    2003015068

Printed in the United States of America

CONTENTS

CHAPTER 1

Types of Writers

Many people think of themselves as writers because they often spend time writing for fun. They may write poetry and short stories or articles for a school newspaper. Actually, anyone who writes could be considered a writer—but not everyone makes a career out of writing. Those who do are known as professional writers, or people who make their living by selling the words they have written.

Authors

The shelves of bookstores and libraries everywhere are filled with books, all of which were written by authors. Just as there are books about every possible topic, there are also different types of authors. Some write **nonfiction** books, which are based on true information and facts. These authors write about everything from **arachnophobia** (fear of spiders) to **Zen** (a branch of Buddhism)

J.K. Rowling signs a copy of her latest Harry Potter book for a fan.

and everything in between. Other authors write **fiction**, or books that are drawn from the writer's imagination rather than facts. Some authors write both fiction and nonfiction books.

Judy Blume is an author who mostly writes fiction. She says that when she was young, she dreamed of being a cowgirl, a detective, a spy, an actress, or a ballerina. She never really planned to become a writer, although as a child she loved to make up stories. When she was older, she began to write her stories down. She says the reason people write is because they have stories inside them that are burning to get out: "The best books come from someplace deep inside. You don't write because you want to, but because you *have* to."[1] As for where she gets her ideas, Blume says they come from everywhere—memories of her life, incidents in her children's lives, what she sees and hears and reads, and most of all, her own imagination.

Poets

Some writers spend much of their time writing poetry. They may write for poetry journals and magazines or publish books of poems. Billy Collins is a well-known American poet who has published six books of poetry. He has also read his poems on national radio and television programs. Collins encourages aspiring poets not only to read poetry but also to memorize it. He says that may seem old-fashioned, but it is the best way to develop a true appreciation for poetry. Also, he says that poets must force themselves to slow down instead of always hurrying and to take time to listen to their inner selves. He shares this advice: "Pay attention not always just to what is on the blackboard, but what is out the window. That bird on a wire. That cloud. Pay attention to the natural world. Pay attention to your daydreams. Pay attention to what is on the periphery, for that is where the small wonders often reside."[2]

Journalists

Newspapers all over the world employ writers, who are also called journalists. These writers often specialize in news about politics, foreign affairs, business, sports, entertainment, or crime. It is their job to find out facts and then write stories about them. It is also important for newspaper writers to make their stories interesting so their audience will want to read them. William Blundell, a writer for the *Wall Street Journal*, says that while newspaper writers must report the truth, they must also be

Poet Billy Collins reads during a poetry fair. Collins encourages poets to read and memorize poetry.

good storytellers. Their articles must grab the readers' attention, hold their interest, and make them remember what they have read. It is not enough to write stories that contain only facts and nothing more, as he explains: "Yes, [the] reader does require specific information, and our first priority is to provide it. But he has deeper and more universal needs that have to be met at the same time or he'll flee. Nothing is easier than to stop reading."[3] Blundell says that making a story interesting is an "unspoken commandment" of journalism that is a common demand of readers everywhere: "For Pete's sake, make it interesting. Tell me a *story*."[4]

Investigating the Facts

Some writers may spend days, weeks, or months digging up little-known facts about a certain issue before writing their stories. These writers are called **investigative journalists**. They perform a valuable function because the things they write can make people aware of important issues. For example, in the early 1970s, two investigative journalists from the *Washington Post* exposed government corruption. Because of their investigation, many top officials were indicted (charged with a crime) and eventually went to prison. The scandal even led to the resignation of Richard Nixon, who was the president of the United States.

Like newspapers, weekly and monthly magazines also have staffs of writers. Alan Hope, a

Investigative journalists discovered information that caused former president Richard Nixon (at podium) to resign.

writer from Belgium, writes for a weekly news-magazine called the *Bulletin*. His stories deal with many different issues, including poverty, housing, crime, and justice. Before he started writing for the magazine, he worked for a newspaper. He says that the biggest difference between newspaper writers and magazine writers is their deadlines, as he explains: "In the old days, I would have an al-most constant deadline. Now that I write for a weekly magazine, the deadlines are less pressing."[5]

A copywriter wrote this simple and funny ad for a billboard.

Advertising Writers

Some writers choose to use their talents to help sell products and services. Advertising **copywriters** write such promotional materials as ads, mailers, and billboards. They also write television and radio commercials. One well-known copywriter is Luke Sullivan, who has worked in advertising for more than twenty-five years. He says the most successful advertising writers are those who are creative and energetic, and who also have a wonderful sense of humor. He believes that people who end up in advertising are often those who are not happy in more traditional jobs, as he explains: "What makes this business great are the knuckleheads. All the people just slightly left of center. This business seems to attract them. . . . All in all, they make for an interesting day at the office, these oddballs, artists, misfits, cartoonists, poets, beatniks, creepy quiet guys, and knuckleheads. . . . It's just one comedian after another all the way down the hallway."[6] Even though advertising is a highly competitive field, Sullivan says there are opportunities for writers who are willing to develop their skills, learn about the business, and work very hard to succeed.

Scriptwriters

Another competitive field is scriptwriting. Some scriptwriters write movies, and others write scripts for television programs. Television networks hire staffs of scriptwriters to write their regular weekly programs. Also, they may use **freelance writers** to write scripts. These are writers who work for themselves.

Most people who are successful scriptwriters worked for many years before being able to sell even one script. For example, Adam Herz, the scriptwriter for the movie *American Pie*, wrote many scripts for popular television comedy shows and tried to sell them. The scripts were rejected, but his writing talent caught the attention of a few agents.

Just a few months after he finished *American Pie*, he had sold the script and the movie was being filmed.

A Variety of Specialties

There are writers who work in many other areas as well. Corporations often employ writers to create publications such as brochures and newsletters. Web-development firms hire writers to write websites. The government hires writers for many different assignments. Some write speeches for top

Bill Cosby (center) uses a script from the *Cosby Show* to help his costar remember her lines.

Some writers prepare speeches for the president and other government officials.

military officials, members of Congress, or the president of the United States. There are also **technical writers** who specialize in writing about technical or scientific subjects. They write manuals for all kinds of products, such as software or computers. They also may write the instructions that come with bicycles, toys, or anything else that says "some assembly required" on the box.

Writers use their talents and skills in many different ways. Some write for television programs, while others write instructions for using laundry soap. A writer's work may appear on the shelves of a local bookstore or be recited aloud during a presidential speech. Or, it may be in the form of a news story that tells the public about an oil spill or a terrorist attack. No matter where writers work or what they write, the words they craft are important. They have the ability to make people laugh or make them cry, to keep them informed and help them to learn.

CHAPTER 2

What It Takes to Be a Writer

The paths writers follow in their careers vary based on what type of writing they do. Most of them attend college and earn a four-year degree. Many study English and other languages and take a number of writing courses. Those who want to pursue careers in newspaper or magazine writing often earn degrees in journalism. Or, some choose to earn degrees in political science, history, law, or geography. This education is valuable because it helps writers broaden their knowledge. However, it is their ability to write well and hold their audience's interest that determines how successful they will be at a writing career.

Professional writers often say that writing has been a hobby from the time they were very

Most writers earn a college degree.

young. As children they wrote stories about their families, friends, and pets. They noticed things that were happening around them and wrote their observations in a journal. Some wrote their own websites, comic books, greeting cards, songs, or neighborhood newspapers.

Clayton Hardiman, a newspaper writer from Muskegon, Michigan, saw writing as a way to escape to new and different places. When he was just six years old, he wrote a poem about his puppy—however, his family had never owned a dog. They were too poor and could not afford to have any pets. Hardiman learned at an early age that writing gave him the ability to imagine whatever he wanted, as he explains: "I discovered that writing was magic. You didn't need money, you just needed an imagination. Whenever I wrote, I could go places I couldn't really afford to go."[7]

The Importance of Reading

Just as writing swept Hardiman away into an imaginary place, he says that reading did the same: "I fell in love with reading when I was very young. And whenever I finished a good book, I would sit there feeling the excitement over where I'd been . . . and ache because there was no more."[8] Most all writers agree that a love of reading and writing go hand in hand. Famous poet Maya Angelou believes reading is so important that parents should read to their babies before they are even born. She says children should be taught to love all kinds of books and stories and poetry, as she explains: "I'll tell you my secret about writing and my encouragement to young men and women: READ. If you want to write, read, and here's a gem of a hint: read and read aloud. Go into your room and hear how your language sounds in your mouth and in your ear. Let it out because poetry in particular is music written for the human voice."[9] Author Stephen King also says that reading is essential for someone who wants to be a writer.

Poet Maya Angelou believes that a love of reading and a love of writing go hand in hand.

In his book *On Writing,* he calls reading "the creative center of a writer's life."[10]

Practice Makes Perfect

Most successful writers, like Stephen King, insist that reading is a crucial part of becoming a writer. They also say that the only way someone can become a better writer is by actually *writing.* Author Natalie Goldberg compares writing with physical exercise such as running. She says that just as people become better runners the more they run, they become better writers the more they write. She explains:

> Some days you don't want to run and you resist every step of the three miles, but you do it anyway. You practice whether you want to or not. You don't wait around for inspiration and a deep desire to run. . . . You just do it. And in the middle of the run, you love it. When you come to the end, you never want to stop. . . . That's how writing is, too. Once you're deep into it, you wonder what took you so long to finally settle down at the desk.[11]

Goldberg's personal goal is to write every day and fill up a notebook once a month. Like her, many writers record their thoughts in journals. They often carry notebooks with them so they can write things down when they are inspired. Jeff Kosloski, a scriptwriter and advertising copywriter from Denver, says that wherever he goes, he always has one or more notebooks with him, and he explains why:

Who knows when I might get a creative idea? There have been many times when I've been driving in my car and this great idea suddenly popped into my head. Obviously when you're driving you can't write, so I just called myself on my cell phone and left a detailed message. I have left ten-minute messages before, describing some great idea that's in my head. Other times I've pulled over on the side of the road so I could jot down a thought in a notebook. The key for me is when I get that simple nugget of an idea, that one little inspiration, then I have to find a way to record it right then.[12]

Kosloski says he also keeps a notebook next to his bed because he never knows when he might think of a great idea for a script—even while he is sleeping.

Not Giving Up

People who write for a living have worked very hard to succeed. Along the way, they have learned many things. One of the most important lessons they learn early on is how to accept criticism and rejection. Successful writers know that even the most successful writers are not liked by everyone. Sometimes they are rejected many times—even for years—before they finally become successful.

No one knows more about rejection than people who write books, stories, and screenplays. Ac-

Many writers record their ideas in journals or notebooks.

cording to the book *Chicken Soup for the Writer's Soul,* many best sellers were rejected when the authors first tried to sell them. For instance, the first children's book written by Dr. Seuss, *And to Think That I Saw It on Mulberry Street,* was rejected by

Dr. Seuss reads *The Cat in the Hat* to a group of children. His first book was rejected twenty-seven times before being published.

twenty-seven publishers before it was accepted. Later, the book sold 6 million copies. As for movies, the script for *Star Wars* was rejected by every studio in Hollywood before it was finally accepted by Twentieth Century Fox. The same was true for *E.T.: The Extraterrestrial, Forrest Gump, Home Alone*, and *Pulp Fiction*—all were rejected at first. Judy Blume offers this advice to aspiring writers:

"Don't let anyone discourage you! Yes, rejection and criticism hurt. Get used to it. Even when you're published you'll have to contend with less than glowing reviews. There is no writer who hasn't suffered."[13]

No two professional writers achieve success exactly the same way. Some knew they wanted to become writers from a very young age, and others did not. Some started out writing poetry and then went to work for newspapers. Some worked at other jobs and wrote movie scripts or books—which they hoped to sell—in their free time. Yet even though writers may follow different career paths, most of them share one thing in common: They cannot imagine a life that does not involve writing.

CHAPTER 3

What Writers Do

Depending on their writing specialty, writers' jobs are often very different. Some are assigned specific topics to write about. Others come up with their own ideas and write about them. There is one task, however, that most writers share in common: research. For instance, travel writers must develop a thorough understanding of the places about which they are writing. So, most spend a great deal of time traveling. Technical writers must become knowledgeable about certain products. If they are writing a how-to manual for a computer, they must learn everything about how the computer works. Then they can write words that make it easy for readers to understand. Speechwriters must conduct lengthy interviews

Fiction author Judy Blume writes almost every day. When she finishes writing one book, she starts another.

with the speakers. They learn what the speakers want to say and the style that is most comfortable and natural for them. They also learn things about the audience so the speech will have the desired effect. Even fiction authors perform research before starting a book. Some may spend a year or several years doing research before they start to write.

Life of a Fiction Author

Judy Blume tries to write seven days a week, even if she only writes for an hour or two each day. Her goal is to keep going until she has a first draft. She usually starts writing about 9:00 A.M. In the past, she rented an office because she thought that might help her accomplish more than if she worked at home. However, her office space was above a bakery, and all day long she could smell fresh-baked bread and pastries. Since she could not get through a day without eating glazed donuts, she decided she would be better off working somewhere else. Now her office is in her home.

Blume says that writing the first draft of a book is always the hardest time for her. She writes during the morning and then often returns to her desk after lunch. She reads over what she has written and sometimes scribbles comments on it. When her manuscript is finished and she begins to edit it, she usually works more intensely and for longer hours. When she is nearing the end of the third draft, she feels a strong urge to get the book finished. That is when it becomes harder and harder for her to leave the story and return to real life. Once she has finished a book and it is in the hands of her publisher, it is common for her to feel sad, as she explains: "It's like having to say good-bye to a close friend. The best therapy is becoming involved with a new project."[14]

A Newspaper Writer's Day

Like Blume, newspaper writer Clayton Hardiman writes most every day. His job, however, is different from that of an author. He rarely has the luxury of focusing on just one story at a time. When he is in the middle of writing about a particular topic, an important lead may come into the newspaper. If that happens, he must stop working on one story and start another. He needs to be able to juggle many different priorities at once, and he explains what this is like: "It's almost like burying yourself in a hole when you're working on a story.

A newspaper writer researches his story on a computer. Newspaper writers may work on several stories at one time.

You're deeply focused on your subject matter. But no matter how much you *want* to focus, you have to switch gears quickly if a higher priority comes along. It's common for me to be working on two or three stories at once. Some snap together in an hour, while others take longer."[15]

No two days are ever the same for Hardiman, and his tasks vary based on what kind of story he is writing. Some require more interviews and background research than others. There are days when he spends much of his time in his car, traveling from interview to interview. Or, he may attend meetings, special events, or jazz concerts. Sometimes he conducts interviews over the telephone. Once he has gathered the information he needs, he returns to the newspaper to write his stories. He says that no matter what types of stories newspaper writers specialize in, there is one thing they all face every single day: deadlines. "I am always working under a tight deadline. No matter how busy I might be, or how many projects I might have on my plate, the newspaper has to come out at the same time each day. That's something that does not change!"[16]

Writing for a Magazine

Alan Hope also faces regular deadlines in his job. But because he works for a weekly newsmagazine, he has a little more time to write his stories than a newspaper writer. Also, unlike

A magazine writer (right) interviews people on the street to gather information for an article.

newspaper writers, Hope's stories do not usually involve "breaking news."

His typical day begins with checking the overnight news on the radio and sometimes the Internet. Later in the afternoon he reads several daily newspapers. As he reviews the various news sources, he looks for story ideas. Then, he does some background research to see if there is enough information available. Once he has chosen what he wants to write about, he approaches the magazine's editor with his ideas. If they are approved, he starts to contact his sources for interviews. When his research is done, he writes the article. Then he reads it over, cutting the length as much as necessary to make the article fit into the magazine's allotted space. The last step is to turn the article in to the editor before his Tuesday morning deadline. Then he starts the process all over again, gathering material for the next week's issue.

Different People, Different Jobs

No two writers are exactly the same, nor are any two writers' jobs exactly the same. Some work for companies or governmental organizations, while others work for newspapers or magazines. Many work for themselves as freelancers. Some write at the same time each day, while others write at all hours of the day and night. One uses a computer to write stories or books, while another uses pads of paper and a fancy gold pen. While there may be vast differences in their jobs, their hours, their techniques, and the words they write, there is one similarity among all writers: The careers they have chosen revolve around the written word.

CHAPTER 4

Meet a Writer

When it comes to writing that makes people laugh, Dave Barry is considered one of the best. He has even been called the funniest man in America. Barry is a humor columnist for the *Miami Herald*. His column is **syndicated**, which means it is published weekly in newspapers all over the United States and other countries. He has also written twenty-four books, and in 1988 he was awarded the **Pulitzer Prize**.

Barry says that when he was young, he never really thought about writing for a living. "I don't recall ever saying 'I want to be a writer' when I was a kid. I didn't know there was such a job as a writer. Even after I started writing, I figured I'd have to do something else to make a living."[17] When Barry was in high school, he was elected "class clown" and he discovered that the things he wrote could make people laugh. So, he began to write humorous articles for his school newspaper. "I wasn't really good at sports, but I was good at being a wise guy. I was a pretty good student—but I also had a big mouth. I liked entertaining my fellow classmates. When I saw that my columns made them laugh, that was all it took to encourage me."[18]

Dave Barry makes many people laugh with his writing.

Throughout his college years at Haverford College, Barry continued writing humorous columns. After graduation, he went to work as a reporter for a small newspaper in West Chester, Pennsylvania. He stayed there for about five years and then left to teach business-writing seminars. In the meantime, he continued to write columns and send them to various newspapers. In 1983 the *Miami Herald* offered him a regular job as a humor columnist.

Inspiration

Barry writes about every possible topic: the government, pets, giant zucchini squash, his daughter's ballet class, potty training, beauty tips, bad habits—actually, there are few topics he has not written about. He says that ideas for his columns come from everywhere: "I get ideas from all around me: other people, the newspapers, television, life in general, my readers. Ideas are everywhere if you just look for them. There are an infinite amount of things to write about, and if you can't find anything, you're not looking around the world enough. It's there. It's all around you."[19] Barry says he most enjoys writing about live events such as the Olympics, political conventions, or the Super Bowl. "If I can write about some specific thing, it's generally easier than when I have to pull ideas out of the air. However, if I need to pull ideas out of the air, I can do that!"[20]

About the qualities that make a good writer, Barry says this: "Someone whose style is readable, natural—and that's a skill that many people don't have. A writer can't copy someone else's style. There are people who are proficient writers, but they're dull. A good writer is someone who makes you want to keep reading."[21] As for whether the ability to write is natural or a learned skill, Barry says it is probably both. "There's no question that some people are naturally good writers and there are also some who will never be. Then there are

Writers look everywhere for ideas. Even the action of the
Super Bowl inspires some writers.

the people who could become better writers if they spent more time reading other people's work. The more you read, the better you will write."[22]

The Daily Routine

Barry writes one newspaper column per week, and his deadline is every Tuesday afternoon. When his column is finished, he moves on to other work such as doing interviews and working on his books. "I always have chapters due and if I don't keep things moving, I can get backed up. If I had nothing else to do—which is never the case—I could finish a book in a couple of months. The time it actually takes is about a year."[23]

When asked how he would describe his job, Barry answers:

To help kids relate to what I do, I tell them this: Imagine that your assignment is to write essays every day. Every day you wake up and walk into the same classroom, and you have to write a new essay. If you don't come up with something new that people want to read, and that you've never written about, and that no one else has written about either, you won't be able to come to class anymore. That's what it's like to do what I do. There's always pressure to come up with a brand new idea and write things that keep people interested and then do it again, and then again, and then again. People might think it's all fun, just dreaming up some hilarious idea, writing about it, and then having everyone read it and tell me how great I am. But it's much more involved than that.[24]

Barry says that there are many times when he does not feel funny, but he still has to come up with humorous things to write about: "I just keep at it and eventually something appears."[25]

The Joys and the Pitfalls

Barry says the pressure is really the hardest part of his job.

It can be tough. Feeling like you're always pressed and you can't ever say "I've got nothing to do for the next few weeks." It's not terrible but it can be tough and it makes relaxing more difficult. Plus, I have to say no to things every day. I'm constantly asked to go places and do things and make personal appearances, and I can't say yes to everything —sometimes I just have to say no. Otherwise I wouldn't have any time for my family or myself.[26]

In spite of the pressure, Barry says that he enjoys his job very much:

I like that I don't have to do the same thing day after day, so it is never boring. I can control what I do, pick my topics, pick my assignments. My job has enabled me to travel all over the world to places like Japan, Norway, England, and France, as well as all over the U.S. I've been able to meet some famous people. Last week I hung out with Steve Martin and Robin Williams—Steve had asked me to help with the Academy Awards this year so I was backstage during the Oscars and met a lot of actors.[27]

Barry says that another good part of his job is his fans. "I've been very lucky to have fans who

Dave Barry speaks to his fans. He urges young people who want to be writers to take writing seriously.

According to Barry, the best training for writers like these journalists is real-world experience.

have bought my books, read my columns—it's very gratifying."[28]

Message for Aspiring Writers

Barry's advice for young people who wish to make a career out of writing is this: "The most important thing is to take it seriously. If you want to be a writer, study what writers actually do. People aren't often aware that this career requires a lot of hard work, and it takes a lot of time to get to the point where someone actually wants you to write for them."[29] Although Barry has a college degree in English, he emphasizes the importance of hands-on experience. "Almost all my journalism education came from actually doing it. While there are no 'standard requirements' for becoming a writer, the very best training is real-world experience. It is so valuable—even more valuable than academic courses."[30]

As for how he feels about his career, Barry says he cannot imagine doing anything else. "It has worked out really well for me. The only advice I ever give to someone who's young and clueless like I was is this: Concentrate on doing what you like to do. If you work hard enough at it, you'll probably learn to do it well. And hopefully you'll be able to find a job somewhere where someone will pay you for doing what you enjoy."[31]

N O T E S

Chapter 1: Types of Writers

1. Judy Blume, *Judy Blume Talks About Writing*. www.judyblume.com.
2. Billy Collins, 2001 commencement address at Choate Rosemary Hall in Wallingford, Connecticut, June 3, 2001. www.choate.edu.
3. William E. Blundell, *The Art and Craft of Feature Writing*. New York: Penguin Books, 1988, p. x.
4. Blundell, *The Art and Craft of Feature Writing*, p. xii.
5. Alan Hope, interview by Peggy J. Parks, May 7, 2003.
6. Luke Sullivan, *Hey Whipple, Squeeze This*. New York: John Wiley & Sons, 1998, p. 231.

Chapter 2: What It Takes to Be a Writer

7. Clayton Hardiman, interview by Peggy J. Parks, August 29, 2001.
8. Hardiman, interview.
9. Luke A. and Kortney R., "Interview with Writer Dr. Maya Angelou," *Teen Ink: Interviews Written by Teens*, September 2001. www.teenink.com.

10. Stephen King, *On Writing: A Memoir of the Craft*. New York: Scribner, 2000, p. 147.
11. Natalie Goldberg, *Writing Down the Bones*. Boston: Shambhala, 1986, p. 11.
12. Jeff Kosloski, interview by Peggy J. Parks, June 2, 2003.
13. Blume, *Judy Blume*.

Chapter 3: What Writers Do

14. Blume, *Judy Blume*.
15. Hardiman, interview.
16. Hardiman, interview.

Chapter 4: Meet a Writer

17. All quotes in Chapter 4: Dave Barry, interview by Peggy J. Parks, May 7, 2003.

GLOSSARY

arachnophobia: An abnormal or irrational fear of spiders.

copywriter: Someone who writes copy for print advertisements and television and radio commercials.

fiction: Any story or book that is based on imagination rather than on fact.

freelance writers: Writers who work for themselves, rather than working for a company or agency.

investigative journalist: A writer whose job is to dig into an issue and uncover the real facts and then write a story revealing what has been found.

nonfiction: Writing based on factual information.

Pulitzer Prize: Awards given annually for achievements in writing in all categories, and music.

syndicated: Something that appears in more than one media outlet, rather than just locally; a few examples include syndicated newspaper columns, syndicated cartoons, and syndicated radio programs.

technical writer: Someone who analyzes and writes about specialized subjects such as computers, engineering, science, or medicine.

Zen: A form of Buddhism that emphasizes meditation.

FOR FURTHER EXPLORATION

Books

Lorraine M. Dahlstrom, *Writing Down the Days: 365 Creative Journaling Ideas for Young People*. Minneapolis: Free Spirit, 2000. A year's worth of creative writing ideas for kids to record in journals.

Ralph J. Fletcher, *Live Writing: Breathing Life into Your Words*. New York: Avon Books, 1999. A book about the "toolbox" that is inside every writer: words, imagination, a love of books, a sense of story, and ideas for how to make the writing come to life.

———, *Poetry Matters: Writing a Poem from the Inside Out*. New York: HarperCollins, 2002. A book designed to give readers an understanding of poetry and to help them write it. Includes interviews with published poets.

Lindsey Fraser and J.K. Rowling, *Conversations with J.K. Rowling*. New York: Scholastic, 2001. The story of the author who writes the famous Harry Potter series. Includes information about her childhood, her struggles, and her career as a writer.

Internet Sources

Luke A. and Kortney R., "Interview with Writer Dr. Maya Angelou," *Teen Ink: Interviews Written by Teens.* www.teenink.com.

Hall of Arts, "Amy Tan: Best-Selling Novelist, Interview," June 28, 1996. www.achievement.org.

Websites

Detroit Free Press, Jobs Page: Your Link to Newspaper Careers (www.freep.com). Includes helpful information of interest to aspiring newspaper writers.

Morton Grove Kids' Public Library Webrary (www.webrary.org). An excellent collection of links for kids who love to read and write.

PBS Kids (www.pbskids.org). An excellent site for young people who are interested in reading and writing. Includes activities, online games, book reviews, and contests for young writers and illustrators.

Stone Soup Magazine (www.stonesoup.com). An online magazine that is entirely created by young writers and artists from all over the world. Young people can read works that have been created by others and submit their own stories, poems, book reviews, and artwork for publication on the site.

INDEX

PICTURE CREDITS

ABOUT THE AUTHOR

Peggy J. Parks holds a bachelor of science degree from Aquinas College in Grand Rapids, Michigan, where she graduated magna cum laude. She is a freelance writer and author who has written a number of books for various Gale Group imprints, including KidHaven Press, Blackbirch Press, and Lucent Books. Parks lives in Muskegon, Michigan, a town that she says inspires her writing because of its location on the shores of Lake Michigan.